To: _____

From: _____

THE HOPE OF Easter

BILL DONAHUE

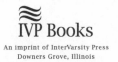

IVP Books

An imprint of InterVarsity Press
Downers Grove, Illinois

InterVarsity Press
P.O. Box 1400, Downers Grove, IL 60515-1426
World Wide Web: www.ivpress.com
E-mail: mail@ivpress.com

Adapted from In the Company of Jesus *©2005 by Bill Donahue*

InterVarsity Press® is the book-publishing division of InterVarsity Christian Fellowship/USA®, a student movement active on campus at hundreds of universities, colleges and schools of nursing in the United States of America, and a member movement of the International Fellowship of Evangelical Students. For information about local and regional activities, write Public Relations Dept., InterVarsity Christian Fellowship/USA, 6400 Schroeder Rd., P.O. Box 7895, Madison, WI 53707-7895, or visit the IVCF website at <www.intervarsity.org>.

Design: Cindy Kiple

Images: iStockphoto.com

ISBN-10: 0-8308-3321-8
ISBN-13: 978-0-8308-3321-4

Printed in the United States of America ∞

Library of Congress Cataloging-in-Publication Data has been requested.

P	16	15	14	13	12	11	10	9	8	7	6	5	4	3	2	1
Y	18	17	16	15	14	13	12	11	10	09	08	07	06			

CONTENTS

INTRODUCTION

Hope. It's a high school senior awaiting an acceptance letter to college; an exhausted single mother of three longing for a husband, a friend or just a good night's sleep; a sales representative counting on a quick recovery from the flu before Friday's presentation to her largest client; an automobile mechanic aching for months of unemployment to end; or a family recovering from a hurricane, clinging to the prospect of a new future while trying to get through the day.

Beyond these physical and emotional obstacles of life lies a deeper, more problematic challenge, one with profound eternal significance. It's a question every person asks in those moments when we ponder the meaning of our lives and the relationships we have with others. It addresses the ultimate relationship: How do I connect with God?

This is no small question. We're taught that God is powerful and good and holy and loving and caring and . . . well, everything we are not. We are weak and not as caring and loving as we should be. And as far as holiness is concerned, let's just say perfection is not a quality our friends would ascribe to us.

Then consider another reality—one that we feel awkward admitting but know to be true to one extent or another. We have rejected God's love, disobeyed God's commands, abused God's planet, and neglected God's people.

So now it is Easter, a season when the story of Jesus and a cross and an empty tomb two thousand years ago is told all around the globe. But for some reason we are not feeling very close to God and wondering if we are worthy of his affection and attention. We ask, "What does he expect from me? How do I connect with God? What will his response be when I talk to him? What about my junk—my faults and sins and failures? What will God think of me when he sees all of that stuff?"

It can be extremely depressing trying to get the "God thing" right.

Extreme circumstances require extreme actions. But what can we do? Where do we get help? How do we find hope again—hope that life will have meaning and purpose; that we will get the most important relationship, the "God thing," right; that we will find freedom from past mistakes, guilt and shame?

That's where Easter comes in. It is a story about something Jesus offers each of us: hope. At Easter, Jesus did something radical—something extreme— so that there would be a reason to hope again. A reason to believe that a relationship with God not only is possible but can be truly amazing and joy-filled.

So read ahead, and get your hopes up!

WANTED: EXTREME FORGIVENESS

After twenty-seven years of unjust and abusive imprisonment in South Africa, Nelson Mandela emerged a hero—a hero with many options.

His people had been oppressed for many years by a foreign white regime, the Dutch Afrikaans National Party, which asserted, *Die wit man moet altyd bans wees* ("The white man must always remain boss"). Under this regime Mandela, a lawyer and political leader trying to bring reform to the country, was charged with treason and ultimately imprisoned.

In prison Mandela suffered mistreatment and humiliation, which he describes in his autobiography *Long Walk to Freedom*. On one occasion he was transferred in the back of a van for about ten hours, shackled to four prisoners. Upon arrival at prison they were stripped of their clothes in a room filled with two inches of water. Their clothes were thrown onto the floor; the men were inspected and then told to dress in the wet clothes.

"The authorities," he continues, "liked to say we received a balanced diet; it was indeed balanced—between the unpalatable and the inedible." "Coffee" was actually ground maize, baked until black and combined with hot water. The bathing and drinking water was brackish, and days were spent hammering rocks and doing hard labor. Often blacks were forced to wear shorts because the authorities wanted them to feel like boys, not men. Mandela protested vigorously and received a pair of long pants—along with a month in solitary confinement.

> I did not see the face or hear the voice of another prisoner. I was locked up for twenty-three hours a day, with thirty minutes of exercise in the morning and again in the afternoon. . . . There was no natural light in my cell; a single bulb burned overhead twenty-four hours a day. . . . I had nothing to read, nothing to write on or with, no one to talk to. The mind begins to turn in on itself, and one desperately wants something outside of oneself on which to fix one's attention. I have known men who have taken half-a-dozen lashes in preference to being locked up alone. After a time in solitary, I relished the company even of the insects in my cell, and found myself on the verge of initiating conversations with a cockroach. . . . Nothing is more dehumanizing than the absence of human companionship.

Despite the harshness, Mandela was spared the worst because of the national exposure his imprisonment provoked. Others were less fortunate, facing the full brunt of brutality and humiliation.

During his imprisonment Mandela was mostly separated from his wife, Winnie, and family, and his people were forcibly moved into townships outside the cities, where there was no plumbing or electricity except for the surveillance lamps high above the streets so helicopters could track criminals at night. There was no education; no one could drive a car. Men had to take buses and taxis to work in menial jobs. Medical clinics were few and ill-equipped, food was scarce, and disease ran rampant.

Put yourself in Mandela's shoes. You've emerged from prison at age seventy-one, having sacrificed the prime of your life for a cause you believe in. Your political party is suddenly strong. Your people are angry and destitute. The white government has squandered your natural resources and mismanaged the funds, handing back a debt-ridden economy on the verge of bankruptcy. What do you do?

Do you spend your remaining years recounting your ordeal and using it as a political weapon to achieve your own ends? Do you incite the angry mobs and hostile youth to rise up? Do you turn the economic tables, forcing whites from their wealthy homes and making them live in squatter camps? Or do you simply evict the whites from the country, even the few who rallied to your cause?

Mandela chose none of this. He was able to continue his fight for a unified Africa and yet not resent his oppressors. "I knew people expected me to harbor anger toward whites. But I had none. . . . I wanted South Africa to see that I loved even my enemies while I hated the system that turned us against one another."

Nelson Mandela ranks near the top of the list of modern-day extreme forgivers. Lewis Smedes, in arguing that we should forgive even those monstrous people who commit atrocities, puts it this way:

> Very ordinary people do extraordinary evil. We need to judge them, surely, and forgive them, if we can, because they are responsible. And because we need to be healed.

Only Satan, argues Smedes, is unforgivable because he is pure evil. To equate even the most despicable person with evil embodied—with Satan—is to dehumanize that person. It removes responsibility from their actions, for now they are nonhuman and thus not accountable. To forgive is to acknowledge their humanity. Or as Henri Nouwen often remarked, "Forgiveness is allowing the other person not to be God"—that is, allowing him or her to be human.

Jesus of Nazareth set the standard for extreme forgiveness. Mistreated, tortured, humiliated, mocked and rejected, he uttered the most remarkable words human ears have ever heard: "Father, forgive them, for they do not know what they are doing" (Luke 23:34).

The words are remarkable for several reasons. Jesus is innocent—even Pontius Pilate, who served as his judge, acknowledged he had committed no crime. He was unjustly tried and sentenced, the victim of false accusers and trumped-up charges. He had the power to destroy those who were crucifying him. His death brought his immediate family only grief and shame.

We all took part in the act of crucifying Jesus. His forgiveness was not directed at a few soldiers and religious leaders; it was—and is—offered to the whole world. Now that's extreme forgiveness.

What does this forgiveness look like in action? To hear "Jesus forgives us" sounds good, but what is the process—what are the ground rules? Are there conditions? Will he withdraw forgiveness if I step out of line? Do I have a role in the process? What does this Jesus expect from me? What is my standing with God in light of what Jesus has done?

Forgiveness is a process. It involves actions by the offended and the offender. When someone wrongs you, you hope they will "own up" to the wrongdoing, admit they were wrong, and do their best not to repeat the offense. It is an act of humility that allows for the wrongful act to be recognized and forgiven, and for the relationship to be restored.

Jesus acts in a similar fashion with us, though you will soon see that his level of forgiveness transcends the human capacity to clean up the mess we have made. He approach is more radical as his relentless love compels him to set things right on our behalf.

First, Jesus hears our confession—he listens at "heart level" for our desire to name the wrongdoing in our life. Then he invites us to turn from old destructive patterns of behavior and enter the wildly freeing process of repentance—a misunderstood and much maligned concept today.

But beyond that, in order to help us set things right with a loving and holy God, he steps in and takes our guilt and shame on himself, cancels the pile of debt that has accumulated for the sins we commit, and sets everything right again. He invites us to enter the process in humility, and then he does all the hard work. Now that is extreme.

So read on, and discover the amazing gift offered to you this Easter season. Prepare to encounter Jesus, the extreme forgiver. There's a reason to hope after all.

1

JESUS HEARS
OUR CONFESSION

Go away from me, Lord; I am a sinful man!

Bill Wilson, the cofounder of Alcoholics Anonymous, was convinced that an alcoholic had to "hit bottom" in order to recover from his addiction. Wilson wrote:

> How privileged we are to understand so well the divine paradox that strength rises from weakness, that humiliation goes before resurrection: that pain is not only the price but the very touchstone of spiritual rebirth.

An alcoholic must confess—that is, agree—that he or she has an unsolvable problem and is beyond hope for recovery apart from outside help. The beauty of AA is that every week, in tens of thousands of groups around the world, such confessions are readily heard and received, without judgment, shame or incredulity.

It is the possibility of mercy, not the fear of retribution, that moves people to genuine confession. A coerced confession is rarely truthful, as people will say anything to escape the threat of pain or judgment. Indeed, lying may delay wrath, but only a sincere confession can evoke mercy.

We experience soul-level freedom every time we admit brokenness, despair and failure in the company of grace-filled mercy-givers. And confessions come easily when wrongdoers are assured of the gracious and merciful response of the one offended.

Do you . . . not realiz[e] that God's kindness leads you toward repentance? (Romans 2:4)

I studied at the University of North Texas for my Ph.D., so I ventured onto the campus several days a month for classes and library research. One day, while crossing the courtyard outside the student center, I heard—and then saw—a man screaming at a group of students. Some were seated on the concrete benches along the perimeter of the square while others sat on the ground, alone or huddled in groups. It was the lunch hour and this was a favorite gathering place to connect with friends and roommates at midday.

It soon became apparent that this man was an angry preacher. He was laying into these college students with a ferocity that I had not seen in many years. Reactions from the small crowd of about thirty were mixed. Some ignored him, some laughed and mocked him, and some appeared angry. But one thing was certain; he was taking no prisoners. His tone was harsh, his mannerisms wooden, his face contorted with rage and his message venomous. "You drunkards and fornicators," he railed. "Do you think you can hide from God? Do you think he doesn't see everything you do in those dormitory rooms at night? The parties, the sex, the drugs?"

Suddenly, my adrenaline kicked in and I found myself standing beside the preacher. Believe me, we were both shocked. I had no prepared message, but I did have something he didn't—the undivided attention of thirty college students. I was angry at his distorted portrayal of truth and sad for these open-minded, truth-seeking students who might never get a glimpse of the real Jesus.

I poured out my heart to these young people, describing the relentless love of God shown to them in Christ, how they mattered to him and how his greatest pleasure would be to become friends with them. I acknowledged that God was holy and that sin destroyed relationships and drove a wedge between us and a loving Creator. But then I spoke of life and hope, forgiveness and freedom.

And then I stepped down, wondering if I had just made a total fool of myself. Feeling awkward and a

bit embarrassed at the whole spectacle, I cut a circu-
itous route away from the crowd toward my class-
room. A student pursued me and asked if we could
talk. The look in his eyes told me this was not going
to be about the weather or some finer point of theol-
ogy. Class would have to wait. We found a bench
and he began.

"Can God really forgive anything?" The eyes of
this twenty-five-year-old student moistened and his
voice began to trail off.

"Yes," I said. "Anything." And then I waited. His
next words caught me totally off-guard.

"I think I murdered my daughter," he mumbled,
staring at the ground between his feet.

As a young pastor I had encountered people with
a variety of problems: addictions, broken marriages,
bankruptcy, homelessness and sexual misconduct.
But murder was new. If there was a time for unconventional wisdom, it was now.

"She was only a few months old," he continued,
"and had a terminal disease that was slowly de-
stroying her digestive system. We fed her with a
tube as her condition worsened. One day, while I
was feeding her . . ." He stopped and fought back
tears. "She died. I think she choked on it. I think I
killed her. Can God forgive that?"

This may sound strange to you, but along with
deep compassion and love for this man, I felt a rush of
joy. Because I could offer him something he could not

obtain for himself—grace. The unmerited and lavish grace of God that Jesus readily dispenses to thousands of people like this man every day. Grace. Something the ranting courtyard speaker had spoken little of.

This was a broken man who needed to know Jesus was an extreme forgiver, a Savior and friend. I doubted he had done anything to cause his daughter's death. It was a terrible tragedy but not of his doing, and I assured him that God's favor rested on him. Now he needed to forgive himself. We embraced, prayed and talked of this loving, merciful and gracious God. He was relieved. A burden had lifted.

Jesus loves to hear a sincere and heartfelt confession. Not because he has a warped sense of power. Not because he needs to prove his omniscience. *I knew it! Did you think you could hide this from me? Who are you kidding?* Not because he's updating the record books. *That's 348 lies for Donahue this year— wow! I can't wait to see his face on judgment day!* Yet many of us have similar views of God with respect to confession. What will Jesus think of us when we tell him what we've done? Oh, intellectually we know that he knows. But it still feels bad.

Confession is an authentic expression of who we are and what we really do, say and think. That's why it's good for us. Confession releases us from self-deception and self-hatred. God doesn't need to hear our confession—he simply longs to. He knows

who we are; it is we who are deceived. To allow
Jesus to hear our confession gives him permission to
heal us. He already has the right and the power to
do so.

I invite you today to approach Jesus as a willing
listener. To pray to him. To have a conversation with
God—a merciful, loving, grace-giving God. Speak-
ing to God in an authentic prayer of confession is
healing and freeing. Brennan Manning describes the
freedom that comes when we honestly agree with
God about our condition. It's a vulnerable but healing place.

> In our struggle with self-hatred, we obviously
> do not like what we see. We find it uncomfort-
> able, if not intolerable, to confront our true
> selves; and so, like runaway slaves, we either
> flee our own reality or manufacture a false
> self—mostly admirable, mildly prepossessing,
> and superficially happy. . . . To pray is to "re-
> turn to ourselves," where God dwells, and to
> accept ownership of our sinfulness, poverty
> and powerlessness. . . . Authentic prayer calls
> us to rigorous honesty, to come out of hiding,
> to quit trying to seem impressive, to acknowl-
> edge our total dependence on God and the re-
> ality of our sinful situation. It is a moment of
> truth when defenses fall and the masks drop in
> an instinctive act of humility.

It's in the moment of confession that God's power, grace and truth are most evident. We confess we need him and belong to him, and we ask him to act on our behalf in ways we cannot achieve for ourselves. And Jesus willingly hears and responds. "If we confess our sins, he is faithful and just and will forgive us our sins and purify us from all unrighteousness" (1 John 1:9). I like that last part—as if forgiveness is not enough, God says he will clean up the whole entire mess.

Can God forgive anything? I've got my hopes pinned on it.

PERSONAL RESPONSE

What would it take for you to get clean? Jesus is willing to hear your confession and to bring healing to your soul. It's a conversation that will change your outlook on life and your relationship with God. To explore this further, consider reading chapter one of 1 John in the Bible.

Or perhaps you want to talk to God. Your mind is filled with questions—your heart is moved to act but you are fearful or confused. It is awkward to admit that we have made a mess of our life, but whatever your thoughts, you can simply express them to God. It might sound something like this:

Dear God, I'm afraid—I guess that's my first confession. I know that you already know everything about me. But it's still hard to put my sin into words. I feel ashamed and disconnected from you. Yet I know that this is the only path to freedom, so I am taking a big leap of faith. Grant me the courage to speak truth to myself and to you. And then help me to rest in the reality that you are the great forgiver, even when it is hard to forgive myself.

2   JESUS INVITES
     OUR REPENTANCE

God, have mercy on me, a sinner.

Repentance. Ugh. Isn't confession hard enough? Why add repentance to the mix? Is it not sufficient to simply name what we've done and agree with God that it's wrong? Confession plus repentance . . . that's almost too much, like choking down cough medicine then rinsing our mouth with vinegar.

Repent. It is not one of the more endearing Bible words. Mothers name their kids Hope or Joy or Grace, but you'll be hard-pressed to find "Repentance Smith" or "William Repentance Owens" on any hospital nursery wristbands. After all, the word conjures up dark images of disheveled men lugging placards up and down the street yelling, "The end is near—repent!"

Does the word really deserve such a bad rap? What

if there's more to repentance than meets the ear?

Perhaps we have such a shallow understanding of the word because we hold such a trivial view of sin. We've given sin an extreme makeover, smothered it with perfume and dressed it in satin and lace. It's almost a beautiful thing these days, celebrated in art, literature and music. Sin has lost its ugliness, its stench. I remember realizing this for the first time when I heard the words of the 1980s hit "Heartbreaker," in which rocker Pat Benatar sings, "You're the right kind of sinner to release my inner fantasies." Hmmm. The right kind of sinner. I guess there are wrong kinds of sinners, too. Axe murderers, child molesters, crack dealers, folks like that. But not fantasy releasers—their brand of sin gets played on the radio.

Don Everts comments that if we ever got a whiff of what sin really smells like, we'd repent—we'd turn and run like a terrified mouse from a stray cat.

> The truth is, knowing the reality of sin—the real smell of it—should not depress and deflate us; it should make us mourn our sins and cry out for help. And crying out, in the kingdom of God, is a beautiful thing. . . . The true smell of sin frees us from the smooth, suffocating lies of this age. . . . Talk of repentance and grace and forgiveness rings hollow if sin is just an arbitrary list of fun things we're not supposed to do.

But that's not the prevailing view, even in the church. I sometimes wonder, where have all the sinners gone? We see lots of offenders who make "errors in judgment" and are "sorry if I've hurt anyone." But confessed sinners? No way. It's more popular to admit to facial reconstruction than to say, "I'm a sinner." It's one of the great anomalies of the twenty-first century—no one sins any more. And consequently, no one repents—no one turns and heads the other direction.

That's sad, because repentance is one of the most freeing concepts in our world. As Everts says, "Crying out is a beautiful thing."

The New Testament word *repentance* means "a change of mind, a turning away." It goes beyond confession to a change of heart and mind that results in changed behavior. It's more than "I'm sorry." The passionate Jesus-follower Paul instructed a church in Corinth about repentance, reminding them that "godly sorrow [for sin] brings repentance that leads to salvation and leaves no regret, but worldly sorrow brings death" (2 Corinthians 7:10). Godly sorrow grieves the heart, alienates us from God and causes a desire to come home, to return. It loves reconciliation, justice and transformation of character. Worldly sorrow expresses sadness over events but makes no determination to pursue internal, lasting changes. Thus it results in death—spiritual, emotional and even physical. Worldly sorrow produces a change in demeanor; godly sorrow produces a change in destination.

Three days before Christmas one year we moved into a sixteen-year-old home in a wonderful neighborhood. The previous owners had severely neglected the property, making the price affordable and renovations considerable. Strangely, during those few days the frigid December temperatures yielded to an almost spring-like fifty degrees. This was great moving weather for December in Chicago.

We couldn't wait to get into the new place. It needed paint, carpeting, minor repairs and some new appliances, but it was home and the view was superb. Our new home rested on a hill next to two small ponds in a neighborhood of about eighty homes. The flat Midwestern terrain allowed us to see for twenty miles out the front windows. There was only one problem. The outside windows had never been cleaned and were coated with a thick gray substance resembling waxed paper. The layers of dirt clouded out the view of the majestic oak trees and shimmering pond across the street. I took advantage of the unseasonable "heat wave" to wash the windows before another freeze set in. Darkness was looming and I was grateful to get most of them clean.

The next morning the sunlight cascaded through the living room, and we had a clear view of the Canada geese lounging beside the pond. The view was resplendent, capturing our hearts and evoking a

sigh from both my wife and me. If it was this beautiful in winter, what would spring and fall be like? I
remembered wondering how the former owners
could sit here day after day, year after year and allow that grime to slowly blur their vision. Especially
with this view! It was beyond reason to me.

Confession says, "Yep, those windows sure are
dirty." Repentance says, "Those windows are dirty,
it's my fault, and it grieves me. I've ignored the problem. But now I'm going to clean them and start pay-
ing attention. When I notice dirt building up again,
I'll get to work immediately rather than feign igno-
rance or pretend the grime will wash itself away."

To identify the dirt of sin and turn from it requires a contrite heart and a change of mind, a new
way of thinking that results in changed behavior.
Jesus invites this kind of contrition, though he is
keenly aware that many of us don't really believe
we sin and therefore do not seek God's grace and
mercy. So, to make it clear and reveal his own heart
about true repentance, he tells us a story, a parable
about a tax collector and a Pharisee who came to the
temple to pray.

The Pharisee, a pious man of high standing, is
self-righteous and proud of his religious accom-
plishments. He strides brashly into the presence of
God and prays about himself. "God, I thank you
that I am not like other men—robbers, evildoers,
adulterers—or even like this tax collector. I fast

twice a week and give a tenth of all I get" (see Luke 18:9-14).

Now there's a humble prayer. *God, thanks that I'm not a loser like these other jokers around here. You must have a hard time even looking at them. I bet you're glad that rule-keeping zealots like me are close by, guys who never miss a service and perform our religious obligations on time, every time. As you know, I work hard at this, above and beyond the call of duty, even fasting more often than our religious system requires. We need more guys like me around this place!*

The tax collector, on the other hand, stands "at a distance" from the worship center, smothered in shame and stricken with guilt. These Jewish outcasts who did Rome's bidding at Israel's expense were a despised and detested lot. "Tax collectors," observes Ken Gire, "were the dung on the sandals of the Jewish community." His head sinks downward, his chin finding its home on his heaving chest. Avoiding eye contact with others he glares at the hardened floor of the temple courtyard, a sandstone mirror reflecting the condition of his heart. Fraud and deceit, trademarks of his business, weigh on his conscience like a millstone around his neck. He desperately wants to reconnect with God but secretly wonders if God will ever receive him. There he lingers on the periphery, feeling unworthy to occupy even two square feet of courtyard space let alone enter the temple itself.

Meanwhile the Pharisee has sized up the competition for religious prominence. It is the hour for prayer and the temple grounds are beginning to fill with the faithful and the sinful. Among the worshipers are the riffraff of Jewish society, the bottom rung on the social ladder—robbers, beggars, lepers and adulterers. *Look at this place,* he thinks to himself. *For goodness' sake, how in the world are we going to keep this place holy with all these people desecrating every square inch of it?*

In his eyes he's a ten in the company of zeroes. No competition today. He stands in the light, but his heart is filled with darkness. He longs for attention. He pauses, delivers his oratory heavenward and promptly justifies himself.

Now the tax collector speaks, not so much with his voice as with the pounding of his fists. The thudding sound envelops his despairing but audible cry. He is overwhelmed with remorse. He slumps, delivers his prayer and humbles himself. He longs not for attention but redemption. Jesus says, "He would not even look up to heaven, but beat his breast and said, 'God, have mercy on me, a sinner.' " Though he stands in the shadows, his heart is filled with light.

Jesus then delivers the kicker:

> I tell you that this man, rather than the other, went home justified before God. For everyone who exalts himself will be humbled, and he who humbles himself will be exalted.

Jesus invites a repentant heart, one that brings the seeker home. God's relentless love motivates that change in heart. An awareness of the destructive and ravaging effects of sin, combined with the gracious love of God, works to woo the broken one home where grace and freedom fill the air. Indeed, it is God's kindness that leads us to repentance.

So what stands in the way? Pride, ego, a foggy windowpane covered with the dust and grime of a past life? It's time to act—to turn around. And Jesus can help you.

PERSONAL RESPONSE

It's often hard to turn from past habits and patterns, especially sinful ones. Reflect for a moment on areas of behavior that are a struggle for you. Are you willing to begin changing some of the patterns and habits that contribute to that behavior? What could you begin to do, in addition to confessing the problem, to turn from behaviors that rob your freedom? Your mind will need ideas and your soul will require encouragement to do this. You might try reading Romans 8:1-17 in a Bible. It will help you understand this better and provide the assurance that God is really for you in this process.

If you are having trouble putting your thoughts to words, consider this kind of prayer.

Jesus, help me to make a 180-degree turn from the activities and behaviors that bind me. I want to change. Help me to find some safe people who will encourage my progress and pray for my resolve. I need to identify activities that will redirect my passions toward fruitful, God-honoring actions and thoughts. Thanks for giving me your Word, your Spirit and the body of Christ—that is, your people—to guide me in this repentance. And help me persevere.

JESUS CANCELS OUR DEBT

For if you forgive [people] when they sin against you,
your heavenly Father will also forgive you.

Stephen Clark owed more money than anyone could imagine—hundreds of millions of dollars. Not only had he mismanaged his own personal fortune, he had borrowed hundreds of millions from Terrance Owens, a multibillionaire oil tycoon and founder of Owens Global Refining & Exploration. Stephen had been hoping to salvage his dying business. Now repayment of the loan was due and he needed more time—lots of it. In reality, he needed a dozen lifetimes to rebuild his business, make it profitable and generate the revenue necessary to write a check for the millions he'd borrowed—not to mention the escalating interest.

As a token gesture of his sincerity to repay the debt, his wife and two sons worked for Owens for free—not exactly the job she wanted after interviewing in the fashion industry. As for his sons, they would rather have stayed in college than work in the office, but there wouldn't be any college anyway now that bankruptcy was imminent. Even with this effort by the family, though, Stephen couldn't put a dent in the amount owed.

"Step into my office, Clark," barked Mr. Owens one Friday morning. "Take a seat." The impressive office was lavishly decorated and contained a mahogany conference table, where a corporate attorney and an accountant sat, looking like they'd just arrived at a funeral.

"Your loan was due last week, and I've waited as long as I can," Owens said. The attorney shuffled some documents while the accountant began some calculations on a laptop computer. "You owe me 274 million."

"Yes sir, I know."

"Plus interest," remarked the accountant, peering over his horn-rimmed glasses.

"So when can I expect payment?" asked Owens.

"I don't know. . . . I . . . I need more time. I think I can really put this together, though. My company is entering into a new venture with a biotechnology firm. They have an experimental hearing device that's a breakthrough in medical technology, and I—"

"Experimental?" huffed Mr. Owens. "Come on, Clark. You're talking about five years before it hits the marketplace and another five before you recoup your investment. I won't see a dime for at least ten years! And who's going to finance your deal when you're 274 million dollars in debt?"

Maybe it was the pressure of the moment, but more likely it was the overwhelming reality that Stephen could never pay this money back. He was emotionally exhausted, his dark eyes and pale skin reflecting the stress he'd carried for months. He was gaunt, having shed thirty pounds from lack of sleep and loss of appetite. Suddenly he burst into tears and slumped onto the table.

For a moment everyone sat stunned. Here was a broken man, a man who had hit bottom so hard the thud could be heard in every office in the building. Mr. Owens had never sat at the table with a man who looked like this. He'd cut billion-dollar deals and fired vice presidents at this table. But he had never watched a man's life unravel before his eyes.

Mr. Owens uncharacteristically found himself feeling pity toward Stephen. Granted, the debt was no small sum, but his Saudi Arabian subsidiary had lost two hundred million dollars in the first year of operation, and another hundred before breaking even. And how about the litigation over drilling rights with the federal government in 1998? He had been cleared of wrongdoing, but six years of court

battles, lost business opportunities and attorneys'
fees had cost him another eighty million. Maybe this
guy's life was as valuable as a court case—and
maybe more so. Oh, what the heck.

"Go home, Clark, and take your family with
you," comforted Mr. Owens, his hand on the weep-
ing man's shoulder. Stephen looked up.

"But sir, it's only 10:30 in the morning and I know
there's so much work—"

"Take them home," Owens interrupted. "They're
done working here. Let them find jobs elsewhere.
Unless they want to stay. In that case, they all need
to report to human resources and get put on the pay-
roll. We can discuss specific salaries later."

"Salaries? I'm confused."

"No—you're forgiven. Your debt is canceled. You
don't owe me a dime. Go rebuild your business."

The silence from the accountant and the attorney's side of the table was deafening. Had Mr.
Owens lost it? Was he going nuts? Did he know how
much of a write-off this was? There were deals in
process in which no one knew the extent of the company's exposure. How could he kiss off almost three
hundred million bucks?

"Clark, did you hear me?" asked Mr. Owens,
looking into the glazed eyes across the table. "Go.
It's okay. Simmons here will draw up the legal papers now and I'll have them delivered to you this af-
ternoon, just to make it all official. Now get out of

here before I change my mind."

"Mr. Owens, I . . . I don't . . . I can't believe . . . thanks, sir. Oh my. Bless you, sir. I'll never forget this. Never."

Stephen and his family practically flew out of the building. They didn't know whether to laugh, cry or scream. At 4 p.m. the papers arrived, notarized with a copy of the loan documents and promissory note with the word "canceled" stamped across the front. All Clark had to do was sign and return the forms to make it official. This was no dream.

The family celebrated that Friday night at the Oasis, a four-star restaurant across town. They hadn't been able to afford something like this in years. In the middle of dinner a man entered and took a seat across the room, apparently waiting for a business associate to arrive. He didn't see Stephen and his family, but Stephen noticed him.

Stan Seevers, a former client, had taken shipment on some equipment—twenty-three thousand dollars' worth—and never paid the invoice because he was sued by an angry competitor just days after the purchase. Seevers needed the equipment to keep the business running while he battled the lawsuit, and he had promised to pay immediately thereafter. Unfortunately, he lost and was forced to declare bankruptcy. All company assets were sold at an auction. Seevers got only ten thousand dollars for the equipment and sent it along to Stephen, but it was thirteen thousand less than the original price.

"Excuse me a minute, honey," Stephen said to his wife as he pushed away from the table. "There's a client over there I want to talk to. I'll be right back."

"Stan? Stan Seevers, right?"

"Yes. And you are . . . ?"

"Stephen Clark, president of Brackford Industries," he said, staring firmly into Seevers's eyes.

Seevers recognized the name and the company and immediately stood. "Uh, nice to meet you, Mr. Clark. Look, about the equipment, I did the best I could when the company folded. Personally, I hope to repay everyone in full some day. But I have to start a new business and it could take a few years. That's why I'm here tonight. I'm meeting a potential partner."

"Potential?" asked Stephen incredulously, his voice rising. "I can't pay my employees and feed my family with potential. I want my money and I want it now!" Now he was yelling. "You think thirteen thousand dollars is nothing? Well, it's a lot of cash to me. It better be in my hands Monday morning, or I'll take you to court myself!"

It was an embarrassing moment, and customers at the surrounding tables were watching. So was Seevers's potential business partner, who had just arrived a few minutes earlier and had witnessed Stephen's angry remarks. Now he approached the table.

"Oh, good evening, Mr. Owens," said Seevers. "I'm sorry about all this commotion. I hope you haven't been waiting long."

Stephen stood frozen in place. *Mr. Owens?*

"Hello, Clark," said Mr. Owens. "I must confess I can't believe what I just heard."

"You two know each other?" asked Seevers.

Stephen stood rigid, suspended in time.

"Not as well as I thought," said Mr. Owens. "Clark, about our discussion this morning. I'm withdrawing the offer. My attorney will be in touch Monday to begin legal proceedings to collect the funds. Now please excuse us. Oh, one more thing—I never want to see you in my building again. You would ruin a man's life for thirteen thousand dollars? Goodbye, Clark. See you in court."

This modern-day parable is similar to a story told by Jesus in Matthew 18:21-35. A servant cannot repay his master an enormous debt. The master demands that the family be sold into slavery and all family assets liquidated to pay the debt, though even this won't scratch the surface. The servant pleads for mercy. The master is moved to pity and miraculously cancels the debt.

When the servant leaves he encounters a fellow servant who owes him about a hundred days' wages, a significant sum for a laborer by first-century standards. Nonetheless it's a pittance compared to the millions he had owed the master. The man asks for mercy but instead the servant has the debtor thrown into prison. Other servants report what happened to the master, who is outraged. "I canceled all that debt of yours because you begged me to. Shouldn't you have had mercy on your fellow servant just as I had on you?" Listen to Jesus' final words in the parable.

> In anger his master turned him over to the jailers to be tortured, until he should pay back all he owed.
>
> This is how my heavenly Father will treat each of you unless you forgive your brother from your heart. (Matthew 18:34-35)

The parable is a moving one. We are the servants with a sin debt we can never repay—not in a million years. We cannot work or buy our way out of it. We can only throw ourselves on the mercy of the one to whom the debt is owed. Thankfully, that one is Jesus, the debt canceler. If we do not appeal to Christ, the consequences are chilling. In the parable, Jesus uses the image of a jailer who tortures the debtor until he can repay the debt. Naturally he cannot—especially when he's in jail. Thus the sentence is eternal.

Jesus is not portraying God as a torturer. This is a parable. Nonetheless, it reveals the disdain God has for those who refuse to have mercy on others after being forgiven such an enormous debt.

The parable raises a few questions. First, have I acknowledged that I have a debt so great I cannot cover it, no matter what I do? Second, do I believe that Christ's death was sufficient to cancel my debt? And third, am I willing to extend mercy to those who have offended me? When they express grief over what they have done, will I forgive them from the heart, never harboring resentment against them? The choice is mine. The choice is yours. "Canceled. Paid in full." Some of the most beautiful words we will ever hear.

PERSONAL RESPONSE

Think for a moment—really think—about the reality that Jesus has paid for and canceled the debt you owe. In light of this reality, what difference will it make in how you relate to God and to people you encounter each day? To help you process this question more fully, consider reading Galatians 2:6—3:4.

I have often been amazed that Jesus moved in to cancel my debt. It has moved me to prayer—to telling God how grateful I am for what Christ has done. My prayer usually sounds something like this:

Dear God, thanks for wiping the slate—no, several slates—clean. Actually, my sins would probably fill a room full of CD-ROMs. And yet it is amazing that you erased them all, even the ones I can't remember, and especially the ones that have caused so much damage. I know I have to deal with the consequences of my sins, but I feel such relief knowing that I will never have to pay the price for them. Thanks, Jesus. I am amazed at the grace and love you have shown to me. What I've been hoping for—a clean slate—is becoming a reality because of you.

Perhaps you want to take a few moments to share similar thoughts with God.

4   JESUS TAKES OUR PUNISHMENT

*I, when I am lifted up from the earth,
will draw all [people] to myself.*

On January 13, 1982, Air Florida Flight 90 departed from what is now Reagan National Airport in Washington, D.C., for Fort Lauderdale. It was 4 p.m., almost two hours past the scheduled departure time thanks to the winter storm that had been pummeling the East Coast all day. The passengers had boarded at 2:45, after which Captain Lawrence Wheaton commanded that de-icing procedures commence. Snow and ice on the ground were so bad that the plane had to be pulled from the gate by a vehicle with chains on its tires.

Finally at 3:59 the plane was cleared for takeoff. The 737 headed down the runway and ascended over the Potomac River. Suddenly, the nose of the plane rose sharply but the aircraft failed to gain altitude. After a brief stall it fell to the ground, striking the Fourteenth Street bridge during rush hour and smashing into several cars. Five people were killed before the plane landed in the icy waters of the Potomac.

I watched the rescue attempts on television. The darkness of the sky and water was broken only by the white fuselage sinking into the water. News cameras revealed a man eerily balancing atop the aircraft. Somehow he had managed to escape the icy waters and had climbed on top of the fuselage, and he was trying to help others out of the water onto the plane. Icy conditions and the location of the plane prohibited any boat from moving quickly to the rescue. So a helicopter was dispatched with a rope ladder. Because of the chafing wind and icy snow, the chopper could hover only briefly above the entombed craft, just long enough for someone standing on top to grab the ladder and be whisked away.

I watched as the man helped the first passenger grab the rope. A few minutes later the helicopter returned, and he helped a second passenger. It was amazing. Then I began to wonder how he was doing this. Certainly hypothermia was setting in. The blustery winds, increased by the speed of the propeller blades, had to be turning his wet clothing into an icy shroud. But he remained steadfast.

The helicopter returned a third time, presumably to rescue him, but he was gone. Likely he was overcome by the weather and slipped into the river, an icy grave for seventy-four Florida-bound travelers that day. Only five survived the tragedy. At least two of them owe their lives to a courageous unidentified passenger. In a way, he took their place—he gave his life for theirs.

Perhaps he expected to survive. Perhaps he thought, *Just one more—I can hold out for just one more.* Or maybe he was one of those rare people who counted the lives of others as greater than his own. We'll never know.

Jesus did not give his life unwillingly. He not only took our place, he took our punishment. And he knew it would happen. Jewish prophets had foretold this seven hundred years earlier.

> We all, like sheep, have gone astray,
>   each of us has turned to his own way;
> and the LORD has laid on him
>   the iniquity of us all. (Isaiah 53:6)

It makes sense to us, or at least we can understand, when someone gives their life for a friend or family member. Or even for a good cause. But it's counterintuitive to sacrifice your life for a meaningless cause or for evil people. Imagine someone willingly forfeiting his life to take the punishment of a Hitler, a Stalin, a Saddam Hussein or a serial killer.

Yet Christ gave his life—took the punishment—for evil people like that. And for evil people like us. Paul makes this clear.

> You see, at just the right time, when we were still powerless, Christ died for the ungodly. Very rarely will anyone die for a righteous man, though for a good man someone might possibly dare to die. But God demonstrates his own love for us in this: While we were still sinners, Christ died for us. (Romans 5:6-8)

Last year on Good Friday our church designed a self-guided, interactive service structured around the traditional seven stations of the cross. Simple instructions were provided to help participants stop and reflect on the symbols at each station. Each pointed to some element of Christ's passion. My family—Gail, Ryan and Kinsley—joined me as we paused at every display, reading the Bible passages provided, praying and pondering. It was deeply personal and moving. Two of the displays especially marked us. One guided us to hold a hammer and spikes similar to those used to nail Jesus to the cross. The other included bread and cups for sharing the sacrament of Communion that Jesus initiated with his disciples the night of his arrest.

I met Christ there in a deeply transforming moment. At first I could only stare at the spikes, my mind conjuring up the vivid images that accompany a crucifixion. Having recently seen Mel Gibson's *The Passion of the Christ*, the scenes were more realistic than they had been previously in my imagination. I heard him panting and pictured his trembling hand, hundreds of onlookers urging me to strike a blow. I put the spikes down after only briefly holding them. And the hammer—my fingerprints were all over it. My hands, pressed downward by the weight of my guilt, made lifting it almost impossible. The realization sunk in of what it really meant for him to "take our punishment." I had to sit down.

The sacrament of Communion also reminded me of the price Jesus paid as he bled and died. When Christians participate in this sacred ceremony, we reconnect with Jesus and his community throughout history. Together we solemnly proclaim that his death brings us life. I felt the guilt falling away and his grace pouring down. Oh I knew I had been forgiven long ago, at age twenty-three when I first experienced the full impact of his amazing grace. But today—on this Good Friday—the sacred act we shared as a family became a declaration of surrender, an act of defiance against pride and ego and self-preservation. I was filled with gratitude and humility, an undeserving rebel basking in the light of a very good God and his extremely forgiving Son. In that moment I returned again to meet Jesus, not just at the foot of the cross, but at the mouth of the empty tomb. I took my part in his death and savored my partnership in his resurrection. We all did. I treasured those moments together—moments of gratitude with my family in the company of Jesus. Moments with some bread, a cup, a hammer and three spikes.

> God, who is rich in mercy, made us alive with Christ even when we were dead in transgressions—it is by grace you have been saved. (Ephesians 2:4-5)

> God made him who had no sin to be sin for us, so that in him we might become the righteousness of God. (2 Corinthians 5:21)

Jesus willingly traded places with us so we could find life. If you're not convinced how incredible that is, just ask the survivors of Flight 90.

PERSONAL RESPONSE

How does it make you feel to know that Jesus stepped in and took your place? What kind of response does that elicit from you? To gain the full import of what Jesus did and how God responds, look at 2 Corinthians 5:11-21. In that passage the Bible describes how God "was reconciling [we might say, reuniting] the world to himself in Christ, not counting people's sins against them" (TNIV). He did not count our sins against us because Christ took them upon himself. As you read that passage, take a moment and reflect on this amazing and extreme action of Jesus.

I know as I reflect on this fully, I often find myself saying something like this:

Dear Jesus, the question that comes to mind is, "Why me?" Why would you step in and take the rap for me? You deserve better than that, and I deserve much worse. What kind of God would allow this? What kind of king would permit this? I can only conclude this: an extremely loving and forgiving one. So here I am, standing in awe of you and with nothing but gratitude.

As you consider what Jesus has done, feel free to express your gratitude to him in your own words. Or, if you cannot fully accept all this yet—if you are still processing these ideas—then simply tell him that. Be real with God, and continue reading. Allow the process to unfold.

5 JESUS RESTORES OUR RELATIONSHIPS

First go and be reconciled to your brother;
then come and offer your gift.

In the A.D. 120s the Roman emperor Hadrian ordered the construction of a wall in Britain down the valleys of the Tyne and Solway rivers. Its purpose was to separate the growing Celtic tribes from the Romans. Though its seventy-six-mile length was impressive, the wall was not large enough to prevent any formidable attack and could easily be breached by a determined army. Nonetheless, Hadrian's Wall had a psychological effect, stemming the flow of people and communication across cultures.

Walls foster a kind of isolationism and self-sufficiency. They always have. Just look at the Great Wall of China and the Berlin Wall. We like barriers—they create a sense of safety and security. "Good fences make good neighbors," goes the saying. But they also drive wedges between people. Years ago we lived in a section of Dallas, Texas, where every backyard was bordered by a six-foot privacy fence. Our personal fortress, backed by an alley that led to our rear-entry garage, fostered isolation, not communication. Most folks hardly saw their neighbors, let alone spoke to them. Personal privacy, not neighborly community, reigned supreme. No one accidentally invaded another's space, and kids and pets were shielded from spontaneous interactions. We were good neighbors indeed, if "good" means self-contained.

And yet, "Something there is that doesn't love a wall," wrote Robert Frost in his poem "The Mending Wall." That "something" is a longing to be connected to God and to others. To be at peace with them. To live in harmony, like members of an orchestra, playing our individual instruments but producing a beautiful composition, the music of community. Walls, though often serving a necessary and meaningful purpose, often remind us of what separates us, what makes us different and distinct. In the kingdom of God, emotional and spiritual walls are barriers to friendship with God and others.

You are all sons of God through faith in Christ Jesus, for all of you who were baptized into Christ have clothed yourselves with Christ.

> There is neither Jew nor Greek, slave nor free,
> male nor female, for you are all one in Christ
> Jesus. (Galatians 3:26-28)

One day the Pharisees, a group that prized separation and threw spiritual wall-building parties on
weekends, approached Jesus to question him about
the Law. One of them asked Jesus to rank the great
commandments in order of importance. Instead of
falling for this trap, Jesus reduced the hundreds of
commands to two, confounding his inquisitors.

> "Love the Lord your God with all your heart
> and with all your soul and with all your
> mind." This is the first and greatest command-
> ment. And the second is like it: "Love your
> neighbor as yourself." All the Law and the
> Prophets hang on these two commandments.
> (Matthew 22:37-40)

In other words, love God and love people—that's
the entire focus of the Mosaic Law and all the pro-
phetic teaching of the Old Testament. Break down
the barriers that keep you from God and people. It is
very simple, yet so profound. Gilbert Bilezikian, a
mentor of mine and founding elder of our church,
often emphasizes the cross as a visible symbol of
Christ's reconciling power.

The cross, in other words, not only provides for
our reconciliation to God in its vertical dimen-

sion, but it also makes possible reconciliation among humans with its horizontal embrace. All the designs of God for the creation of the new community are achieved through the cross.

Paul writes in Ephesians 2:13-16 that those of us who were far away from God and one another are "brought near through the blood of Christ," and "through the cross" he reconciled us into one body. God desires oneness with us and wants the same for the people he created, beginning with the Jews and non-Jews of Jesus' day. Paul explains how through Christ, God "has made the two one and has destroyed the barrier, the dividing wall of hostility" and that "his purpose was to create in himself one new man out of the two [Jew and Gentile], thus making peace, and in this one body to reconcile both of them to God through the cross, by which he put to death their hostility."

I returned to my high school's twentieth reunion a few years ago, anticipating that I'd see the effects of aging and maturity (or lack thereof) among the returning alumni. Such reunions are a kind of rite of passage for all who attend. As Gail and I arrived at the hotel, I wondered if Karen would be there. No, she wasn't an ex-girlfriend. Karen was someone I had played a rude trick on at a party, embarrassing her in front of dozens of classmates.

Put simply, I made her the brunt of some crude juvenile humor as part of my ongoing ploy to entertain people and get attention—this was before my life-changing encounter with Jesus. My stunt caused her to run crying from the party as I and my friends roared with laughter. That was the last time I had spoken to her. Now, as I entered this party twenty years later, there sat Karen. Gail, who knew the story, knew what I had to do. And so did I.

After settling in and greeting some of my old buddies, I walked over to her table. "Hi, Karen."

"Hello, Bill. Welcome back."

"I wanted to talk to you about something that happened a long time ago," I said. "I don't know if you remember . . ."

Before I even finished the sentence she remarked, "Oh, I remember." Of course, how could she forget?

"What I did to you was really terrible, and I'm sorry." She nodded and offered a cautious smile as if to say, "I appreciate that."

"This may not mean much to you," I added, "but I have come to know God in a very personal way, and he has done much to change my heart over these years. I have a long way to go, but I wanted you to know that I'm ashamed at my behavior and hope that someday you can forgive me. That's all. I hope you enjoy the reunion."

She was a bit startled but felt my sincerity. "Thanks, Bill. Thanks for saying that."

As I walked away I felt a new freedom. I had been forgiven by Jesus, but now this relationship, broken by foolish sin, had been restored, at least as much as possible. I don't know if she ever fully forgave me, but I was free. I had been reconciled. Though our relationship had never been close, it was important to me—and to Christ—that I do my best to make it right. I felt the joy of heaven and the affirmation of my Jesus, the one who understands the power of forgiveness and the freedom that comes when wrongs are righted and "those who are afar" are reconciled.

Jesus still meets me here often—at the crossbeam of reconciliation. That's because I sin often and drive wedges into my relationship with him and others. His love and grace provoke me to come clean with him and to heal rifts with people I love.

Our God is relational, and the destruction of authentic, loving relationships grieves him because it erects a wall of separation. The Bible is clear—sin alienates us from God and one another. Jesus came to reconcile us with God and restore our connection with each other. The cross was the means of reconciliation. His death brings us together—across racial, ethnic, religious and national barriers. And now we can truly be in the company of Jesus, enjoying fellowship with people and friendship with God.

Our choice is to do the work of Christ and be wall-breakers or to destroy that work and become wall-builders.

I'd rather walk across the room and be a wall-breaker.

PERSONAL RESPONSE

Look back at relationships you've had. What makes the good ones thrive and others fail? When there is relational breakdown, what does it take to put it back together? Now reflect on your relationship with God. Are you aware of everything he has done to make a vibrant relationship possible? Consider reading chapter two in the book of Ephesians, a letter to a church that was struggling with relationships with God and with one another. It will provide some further insights for you. Or ponder this statement in 2 Corinthians 5:18 in Eugene Peterson's paraphrase of the Bible titled *The Message:*

> All this comes from the God who settled the relationship between us and him, and then called us to settle our relationships with each other.

A FINAL PRAYER

Perhaps after reading this you have grasped what the extreme forgiveness of Jesus has accomplished for all who desire friendship with God and others. This would be a good time to pause and thank him. I found these words forming in my soul and wanted to express them to God. Take a moment to gather your thoughts and freely express them to the God who has done so much—even taken such extreme measures—to restore his relationship with you.

Thanks, Jesus, for being the glue in my relationships, especially between me and my Father in heaven. And thank you for doing the hard work of reconciliation so that all people who call on your name can enjoy unity, putting away prideful differences and petty resentments. And help me to notice when I re-enlist in the wall-building business. I'd rather tear some down, but I can drift into old habits easily. I need you and some good friends who can keep me on the path. You are so good.

Jesus promises that your prayer will be heard. Simple, truthful words from you are music to his ears. Express them honestly and directly. He can handle whatever you need to say, and he will meet you in that prayer. Trust him. Put your hope in what he has done and what he has promised. You will find your relationship with God restored, and your relationships with others deepening.

There is now new freedom in Christ to experience the full life that he promises. You have admitted your sin and turned toward God. Jesus has taken your punishment and canceled the sin debt, restoring the broken relationship between you and God. Life starts over! You have new hope!

Jesus has taken extreme measures to secure your forgiveness and to offer the hope of a new relationship with God. But that is just the beginning. With this new relationship comes new possibilities and hope for a meaningful future. Jesus did not simply walk into the loan office of a local bank and pay off your sin debt like a homeowner pays off a mortgage. He wants to know you and guide you, to enjoy your company for the long haul.

In addition to experiencing Jesus as the extreme forgiver, there is more to a relationship with him. This booklet was just a portion of the material found in the book *In the Company of Jesus*, written to help you experience Jesus and the life he offers. The book will guide you in your journey to discover more of this Jesus. In its pages you will meet him not only as an extreme forgiver but as

- a *relentless lover* who never stops giving away his love

- a *provocative teacher* who shapes your thinking with truth and grace

- a *sacred friend* who walks with you through life's joys and trials

- a *compassionate healer* who binds your wounds and embraces your sorrows

- an *authentic leader* who guides you with integrity and confidence

- a *truthful revealer* who opens your mind to a clearer picture of reality

- a *supreme conqueror* who helps you face your future with courage

I continue to experience Jesus in these ways and hope that you will discover the same. I pray that this Easter marks a new beginning for you; a new life in Christ who is eager to show you the incredible life God has prepared for all who seek him with all their hearts. This is the hope of Easter.

May he bless and guide your journey, and may you experience all the fullness of God. Then this will truly be a happy Easter.

NOTES

Introduction

p. 9   *Die wit man:* Nelson Mandela, *Long Walk to Free-dom* (Boston: Back Bay Books, 1994), p. 111.

p. 10   "The authorities": Ibid., p. 392.

p. 10   "I did not see the face": Ibid., p. 334.

p. 12   "I knew people": Ibid., p. 568.

p. 12   "Very ordinary people": Lewis Smedes, *Forgive and Forget* (New York: Simon & Schuster, 1984), p. 109.

Chapter One: Jesus Hears Our Confession

p. 15   "How privileged we are": Quoted by Philip Yancey, "Lessons from Rock Bottom," *Christianity Today,* July 10, 2000, p. 72.

p. 20   "In our struggle with self-hatred": Brennan Manning, *A Glimpse of Jesus* (San Francisco: Harper-SanFrancisco, 2003), pp. 86-87.

Chapter Two: Jesus Invites Our Repentance

p. 24   "The truth is": Don Everts, *The Smell of Sin* (Downers Grove, Ill.: InterVarsity Press, 2003), pp. 93, 95.

p. 28   "Tax collectors were the dung": Ken Gire, *Instructive Moments with the Savior* (Grand Rapids: Zondervan, 1992), p. 35.

Chapter Five: Jesus Restores Our Relationships

p. 51   In the A.D. 120s: Ted Olsen, *Christianity and the Celts* (Downers Grove, Ill.: InterVarsity Press, 2003), p. 37.

p. 53   "The cross, in other words": Gilbert Bilezikian, *Community 101* (Grand Rapids: Zondervan, 1993), pp. 34-35.

UNCONVENTIONAL WISDOM
AND UNEXPECTED HOPE

The Hope of Easter is adapted from portions of the book *In the Company of Jesus: Finding Unconventional Wisdom and Unexpected Hope* by Bill Donahue.

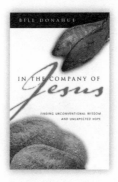

This winsome approach to Jesus will expand your ideas about who he is and draw you into his very presence. Written in forty brief segments with opportunities for personal reflection and dialogue with God, *In the Company of Jesus* makes ideal daily reading and serves as a companion to the **Jesus 101 Bible Study Series.**

The eight guides that make up the **Jesus 101 Bible Study Series** offer you a fresh perspective on who Jesus is, how he related to the people around him and how he interacts with you today. This series is designed by small group expert Bill Donahue. Each session includes quotes and questions to get you thinking, an inductive Bible study, an opportunity to connect your story with Jesus' story, and ideas for taking the "next step" in your journey with Jesus.

Individual titles in the **Jesus 101** series look at the character of Jesus from eight different perspectives:

- Authentic Leader
- Compassionate Healer
- Extreme Forgiver
- Provocative Teacher

- Relentless Lover
- Sacred Friend
- Supreme Conqueror
- Truthful Revealer

As you spend time in the **Jesus 101 Bible Study Series** or the companion book *In the Company of Jesus,* you'll discover how Jesus fulfills your deepest needs and desires. And you'll fall in love with him—for the first time or all over again.